the fruits of her bittersweet sadness, left to rot

a poetry & prose collection

by leta iris

illustrated

by sadie rose

MADNESS – FEMININE RAGE

> the bitterness, the sickness, the rage.

HUNGER – CRAVING DESIRE

> the ache, the burn, the need to devour.

EARTH – BONES BURIED

> the acceptance, the existing, the roots.

THIS POETRY COLLECTION IS BEST SERVED

NEXT TO A PULSATING, RAW HEART,

ALONGSIDE YOUR STOLEN GIRLHOOD

AND CHIPPED BABY TEETH.

leta iris, author of *when summer fades to fall,* reveals her own experience of girlhood within her second collection, *the fruits of her bittersweet sadness, left to rot.* this piece presses on the aching bruise within her melancholy and allows it to bleed deep colors of truth. this visceral collection explores the feminine bite, each diary-like entry a tribute to the inner child. the three components of the book, "MADNESS," "HUNGER," & "EARTH," feature a rawness that many fear to reveal. an ode to brokenness, a desire to be seen and devoured, and a spiritual calling to become one with nature. if sylvia plath sings to each aching fragment of your soul, this collection is yearning to cradle your younger self and caress your cosmic heart.

the fruits of her bittersweet sadness, left to rot

the fruits of her bittersweet sadness, left to rot

MADNESS

THE END OF SUMMER SMELLS LIKE CHARCOALED GRIEF /

scraped my knees / from crawling / my way /
through the turmoil / of my mind, / left a
bloodied trail / dripping on the earth. /
 i will gut everything / that i am / if it means that /
i can start over, / to climb inside / the stickiness /
of my mother's womb. / a suffocating warmth /
where i may rest / for a while. / my existence
is a tomb, / confined / to vampirism. / i have
become / the darkness, / i am cold once again. /
blackened frostbite / in the heat of peak july, /
i am still picking the rocks / from the crevices /
of my skin. / i wasted august / trying to find
myself, / my brittle bones / are shriveled. / hungry
/ for a feeling / i've not quite / tasted / yet. /
starved / for the newness of september /

A SYLVIA PLATH SORT OF
BLISTERING, INCURABLE ACHE.

a "mad girl's love song" sickness
that cannot mend with time
or medicine, a   disconnect
from the earth. the wires
are softly sparking, but still   sev   ered.
unable to withstand the rushing current
of my daily life, even simple tasks drain
my veins and i can't feel   a thing.
the numbness rots each vessel in my brain,
time passes by and my organs twist.
my figs have splattered onto the dirt,
my opportunity growing mold and
            d i s i n t e g r a t i n g.
my mind is   detached,   tingling
but lifeless as a limp leg as it falls
asleep. the sensory awareness of my life
is still there, somewhere. only far,
far away from where i dwell. the bruise
that pulsates in my hippocampus,
depleting me from joy. an open wound
of !!! madness !!!, {{{ spiraling }}} into
sickly poetry and a sense of impending doom.
it crusts, it peels, it lingers.
a deep abyss, a **black**   **hole**
of questions and empty diagnoses
and an ache to be understood, to be free.

THE MAGGOTS CRAVE
MY SORROW

my ribcage echoes with a guilty conscious. / the child inside of me was told that she was born sinful, / created with the promise of death. / still i beg for forgiveness for the earthly flaws / that i did not choose, / can not escape from. / divorcing my mistakes and seeking rebirth, / yet i will never be cleansed. / all of the pharisees are still pointing bony fingers / of blame at me, / putting themselves on / pedestals next to godliness. / but i found true holiness within the dirt, / beside the humility of earthworms and roots. / i offer the sacrifice of my decaying bones / to the hungry maggots, / they feast on my brain / and find their bellies / full of my sorrow. / my imperfections reflect my humanity, i recognize that my impurity is apart of my being. i am not guilty nor innocent, i simply am. i am the rage of burnt witches, i am intense, i am the wind, i am the sea, i am cosmic, i am. /

the fruits of her bittersweet sadness, left to rot

A CARNIVOROUS,
CANINE OF A WOMAN

i am but a vessel of
a starved, angry dog
that lives behind my jagged
teeth. hungry, stomach
ravenous for the violence
that haunts my blood-
a wild obsession,
carnivorous instinct.

every molecule in me
screams- angry, with revenge.
i ache to escape the cage
of my own mind, forever
tortured by the guard
of my own heart. one
can only trust so much,
until there is nothing left
of me to misuse. to devour.

my bark, a warning. my howl,
a plea. a defense mechanism
to keep away. only few tend
to understand me, to stay.
afraid of my bared teeth
and eternal rage. i am
too much for most.

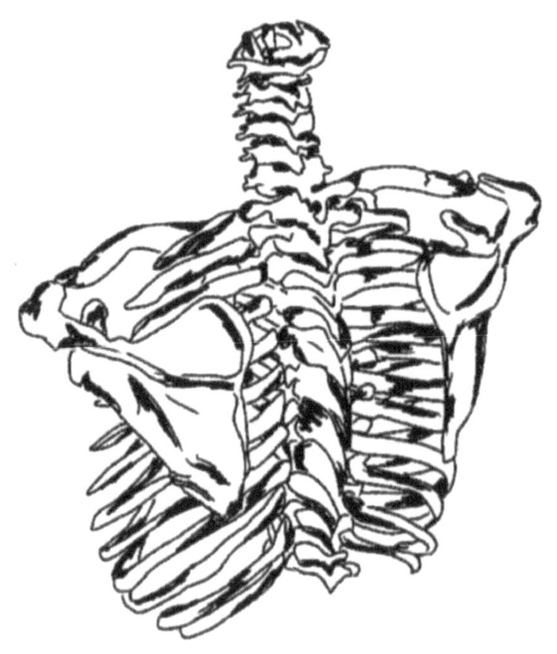

THE EXOSKELETON OF
A HYSTERICAL WOMAN

// i am insectile / heartless / numb /
existing. / words crawling up my throat
but leaking out as a pathetic choke /
a wilted cough. / i hate
that they can see me / perceive me. /
don't try to define me / i can't
even tell you who i am anymore. /
don't ask me how i've been /
i just exist / i have no memory /
my life is just a blur of survival. /

/ i clip my own wings / to hide beneath
layers of an epidermis i am ashamed of /
a mask of different personas. /
my spine twisted / from morphing /
into someone new / plucking out
each feather / of who i was / my skin
is cursed by the delusional battle
with own mind. / maybe i am
subhuman / an alien. / i yearn
to be one with the smoke / invisible
but still alive. //

II OF PENTACLES, EARTH
[REVERSED]

juggling the priorities of
my life, to an endless cycle of
           t r y i n g
to catch each element and make
it do tricks. to impress, to prove i am
doing it (life) right, an example.
the eldest daughter inside
of me dictates my ritualistic
hunger to succeed,
to mean something.
each all fall and splatter
on the ground, one by one
like spoiled plums, purple ooze
staining the earth below me

fruit flies circling to devour
my potential as i lap up any
remnants of the spoiled, moldy
fruits of my wasted labor. dirt
on my tongue, seeds between
my teeth. fists clenched, knuckles
bruised from grasping onto the
flesh of my life until it seeps into
the concrete and i am just left with
the pit, the center. me. at the core,
i am stripped bare, an echo
in a hollow body.

previously published in the autumn 2025
edition of South Broadway Press

i feel as if i am otherworldly, / a celestial fragment / that cascaded to the earth below, / an asteroid of knotted flesh. / disconnected / from worldly affairs, / my mind forever dwelling in the sky, / with the fowl and cloudy abyss. / i fear that i am too conscious, / too aware of my own breathing / and place holding / within the universe, / my inevitable death / and unknown fate. / i watch my life from the sidelines, / a passenger of a never-ending train, / auburn trees whisking by / like a blurry stretch of film. / my eyes of empty blue / hold a permanent glaze, / an unawareness / of my physical presence, / that they can see me. / interpret me. / judge me. / i long to blend in / within the smoke, / invisible to everything / but the darkness, / the light, the ghosts.

RECIPE FOR THE ELDEST DAUGHTER

serving size: enough for everyone

- a heaping cup of rage, over pour
- a pinch of sea salt
- eyeball a scoop of your mother's servant heart
  and your father's sacrifice, stir
- half/full optimism, beaten by betrayal
  into half/empty pessimism
- caffeine and liquor: unhealthy amounts of tea
  and coffee and wine and amaretto
- a teaspoon of shattered savior complex
- expired empathy for the evil
- molded figs, gathered from the carpet of my
  childhood home, wasting away in the
  basement of my potential
- 3/4's cup tomboy, but your father has no sons.
  the lineage, the family line dies with you
- a desire to protect your younger sister from the
  world, because no one protected you
- addictive tendencies, to substance and boys
  and attention and that i seldom received
- long sweaters and bandanas and bandaids to
  cover the carved skin and plucked hair and
  peeled skin of your anxiety, a fucked-up way to
  plea, to release, to get them to finally notice
- undiagnosed childhood mental illness, substitute
  for apothecary healing and diligent prayer, fail

GROCERY LIST FOR BRUNCH WITH MY MOTHER, MY PAST SELF, & MY FUTURE DAUGHTER

-a blood orange,

        to   sp / lit   three ways

-guilt, my mother's lingering

        narration

          of my life

-a knife, to   divide   my life into

        p i e c e s   and give them
each a   s l i c e

-wings, feathered, preferably from a raven, to mourn the
loss, the   disconnect   from my past self

-a wishbone, to pick the potential from my teeth and
wish on my future

-midnight stars from my hometown, evolved into 4 am
insomnia of city lights

-incense, to b u r n   away all evil spirits except for
my   own

-a bottle of rainwater, or river water- whichever is
cheaper, to anoint

- [a hedge of protection,] my mother always prays for one over my family

-freshly rolled and lit tobacco, cancerous and addictive… sometimes i miss the smell of my father's
        way to cope

-wine, to drown my sorrows
        but i'm not an alcoholic [??]

-my dna, my genetic code, my generational curse….

INESCAPABLE

-roots from the tree of life, maybe they can save me ?!!! save her !!?

-the book of revelation, to read during my existential crisis to send me

— further ——

s

        p

            i

                r

                    a

                        l

                    i

                        n

                    g

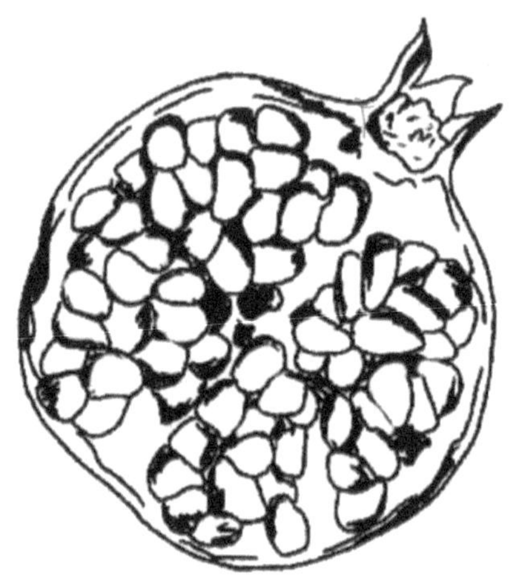

WHAT'S IN MY PURSE (EMOTIONAL BAGGAGE)

AS A 21-YEAR-OLD GIRL IN A CONSTANT IDENTITY CRISIS

// pomegranate & fig seeds / a tarot deck & a bible & crystals & a rosary because i don't know what the fuck i believe in, but i crave to believe in something (there has to be something after death, right? it had to all have been worth something?? right?? god, i'm spiraling / ashes from my childhood dog + a loose cigarette / a tiny notebook for scribbles & profound thoughts that i may never share / sea salt because i constantly feel faint / the literal moon / "seasonal" depression that lingers during all four seasons / marina & the diamond's entire discography / a failed taxidermy lamb / maternal instincts with no desire to be a mother / the fear of death without being remembered / rushing currents of a heightened ego, then self-deprecation / (i'm better than them but apparently i hate myself) / a singular silver hoop earring, the matching half probably in a gutter or buried in the leaves from three summers ago / a hair-tie from my ex best friend, still in the shape of her wrist (i can't let them both go) / my uterus disguised as a sylvia plath poem because apparently i have to hide that shit from male politicians, surely they can't comprehend the fig tree analogy / cannibalism metaphors for love, a violent expression of desire and devotion //

THE FIVE STAGES OF GETTING OVER HER
[GRIEVING THE DEATH OF THE LIVING]

1. cry. wail, even. cough up blood and tear up photos. relentlessly piece them back together with glue that just won't fucking stick. *even when i beg.*

2. understand that we were destined to fail. doomed from the beginning, but i burned for it still. we were never written in the stars, but i wrote your name on the headstone that you buried my broken body beneath.

3. reflect on the destructive, parasitic infestation that was the reality of us. the invasive mold growing under our surface. manipulating, infecting me until i became a sickly corpse. you were the tumor and i was the zombie, blindly trusting that you had the best intentions. *that i was a valuable host,* losing less and less of myself, until i was nothing.

4. become a *body robbed of its soul.* numb, rotting away. summer leaves wilted and clipped, dehydrated from the emptiness of forever winter. i wonder if you laugh about how ill i am.
    how sick you've made me.

5. i'm not quite sure what comes after four. i don't know if i ever will. the naivety in me, *waiting like a shelter dog* at the rusted gates, abandoned by its owner. kept alive by the shard of hope that you'd want me again. that you'd crawl back and reignite a bruise that i craved the absent agony of.

SHE WAS NOT PLACED ON THIS EARTH
TO BE SUBTLE.

she is a thunderstorm; a loud laugh, a drunk
walk home in maroon high heels.
a marijuana infused car, a jumbled chime
of keychains, an alanis morissette song,
a bold lipstick. she is harsh.

her teeth are permanently grit
from biting her tongue, jaw clenched
from holding back tears and an obnoxious
accumulation of "fucks." blunt bangs
and unwanted truths, she will never be accused
of being a fake bitch. she may not be liked,
but she will never be a liar.

her eyeliner is always smoked and sharp,
brows always furrowed because she can
never hide her judgmental facial expressions.
an angry daughter, content with being the
black sheep, the outcast, the misfit.
she was not made for most.

despite her harshness, she can also be soft.
she loves very deeply, she hates very deeply,
every emotion consumes her like a bodily plague.
like a tsunami, like a stroke. she cannot
be contained, cannot be tamed.

the fruits of her bittersweet sadness, left to rot

MY MAN CAVE

i wouldn't have heads of deer plastered on my wall, or
game i've slaughtered. my prizes are men i've hunted,
men that targeted me as their prey. with fake glass eyes,
tongues removed. so they can no longer see me, taunt
me. taxidermied, frozen in time. stuck in the position
that they once put me in. helpless, vulnerable, weak.
they gave me no other choice but to bare my teeth, *gums
swollen with the venom.* i've been waiting. *revenge looks
so sweet* on the peeling florals of my wallpaper.

there would be a dusty recliner from a flea market in the
corner, stained in the blood of past lovers and my own.
from fighting. instead of empty whiskey bottles, i would
have wine. vials of love spells, cursed potions. bottles of
teeth and *jars of the hearts that broke my own.*

a hand me down box tv replaying miranda lambert.
a dart game of rusted knives, thrown at polaroids of
old friends, new enemies. *my ashtray is my own throat.*
i *swallow the burn* as i *swallow my own pride.*
an upside-down flag. the red, white and blue blurred to
purple, as i squint in anger. life spent spinning in circles,
in fear. because *i am no longer safe* when i step outside
my cave. i have never been safe.

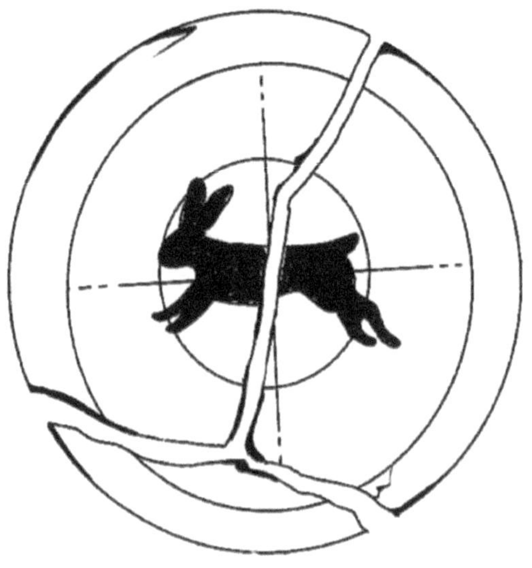

A WOMAN, SCORNED BY THIS WORLD

my life is not 'aesthetic'
      not robotic,
      defined by a glass screen
      where beauty is altered
      and curated
          defined

i am only human, a twenty-something girl
      with stubble on her bruised ankles
      chipped, uneven, coffee-stained teeth
      overgrown roots from black box dye
      frizzy, tangled morning hair
      bitten, unpainted nails

in a world where normal is boring
      unique is judged
      trendy is basic
      too much is trashy
      too little is lazy
      messy is crazy

a society where the standards choke women
      leash them
      train them to hide
      shame them when they shine
      name them
          "slut"
              "bitch"
                  "whore"
                     "cunt"
                "tramp"
             "skank"

i can never just exist
     just *be*
without being
     observed
each flaw,
     recorded
     remembered
and i am so full
of rage,   **exploding**
boiling over
but only seen as
     "hormonal"
not justified
seen at eye level
i am always

below.

     i am exhausted
     the bruise has been pressed
     poked, prodded
     so often that
     i just don't care
anymore.
i am content,
able to breathe
     by just being myself
     a scorned woman
     with nothing left to give
     nothing left to keep
     but
     myself

FERAL FEMALE

she is a feral female / her purse is fifty pounds of
mystery / she glares back at staring men instead of
ignoring them / braless, nipples through a white tshirt / a
drunk cigarette / unapologetically herself / impulsive /
she dwells "outside the box" / defined by what sets her
soul on fire / she has a bitter bite / a swollen heart, barely
beating / but beating nonetheless / dripping poisonous
honey from her lips / she may be cruel, but at least she's
not a fucking liar. / jealousy is a rotten disease / flies
swarm / bite marks line her arms / yet she persists. / only
few understand her / but those who choose to stay / she
will brand their names on her psyche / with a rod of iron
loyalty. / she is a cathedral / a place of worship /
a religion.

THIS WORLD HAS WITHERED, WARPED MY GIRLHOOD

i buried my baby teeth in my garden,
they grew into carnations
ivory petals of my innocence
womanhood barely budding,
yet my girlhood was swallowed whole

vultures hovered at five years old,
flossing the fresh blood from my
empty gums. he who stole the taste
of my naivety by the water fountain
purity quickly stained, washed red
in the river of warped sexuality
forced to carry my own cross
before i even knew what sin was

i became aware of my own
body far too early, never
truly owning it. claimed
by lust and perversion, dictated
by shame and avoidance of mirrors.
reflection shattered, glass shards
buried deep in my knuckles

irremovable, unable to repent
to be washed clean of myself
my trauma blossomed into
a withered reality, flowers
fearful of touch- even by
the gentlest of gardeners

EXIT WOUNDS OF MY INDEPENDENCE

you peel each layer of my skin with the cruelty of your words, slowly. the desire to control. the blood orange tanginess of my spirit, withering at every wedge under your criticism of my being. the acidic strength of my independence rotting away, dissolving beneath the pressure of bleach that you press into my sorry soul.

to cleanse whatever uncontrollable evil that lives behind the surface of these walls, a creature wearing me as a meat suit- living off vodka, blood cells, caffeine, fingernails, and pomegranate seeds. you detest the nasty embrace of my womanhood. i am raw, dirty, honest, loud. i make insecure, uneasy men uncomfortable.

each passive comment of cruelty you make is a jab at my open bullet wound. you needed an escape route from the galaxy girl- an alien you were afraid of, needing to control. to chain her down with rusted barbed wire to your simple earth, where you are god. i hope the venom from my feral feminine bite eats your ego away, tearing the flesh from the bone as my memory gnaws at your narrative forever.

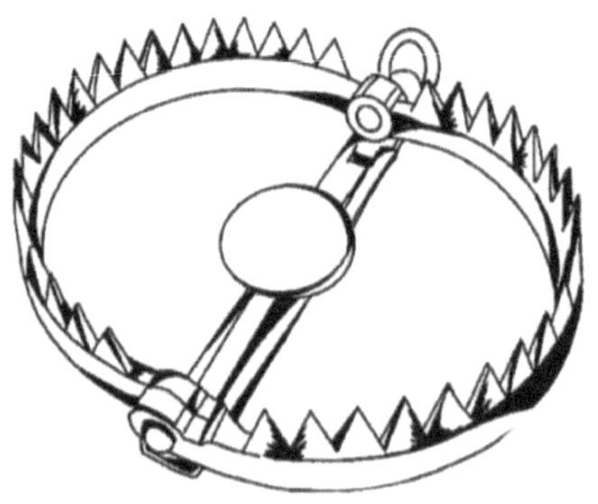

[ZOOCHOSIS]
WITHIN MY OWN BODY

insanity, an ache to creep
from this mind, this cage.
to rip my soul from my skin
peeling layers of perception
and   levitate
philosophical pessimism
cursed consciousness

i am too aware of
my own   existence
my own   eternal fate,
my own   impending
        doom

the mind   detached
        from the body
a life with a permanent s p i r a l
anticipatory expiration

a desire to   die
a fear of   death

MY BODY IS NOT A TEMPLE, BUT A CIRCUS

ACT I

juggling normal expectancies while navigating
the inescapable, revolving demands of
dysautonomia. every day is a performance.
a façade, masking my crumbling body.

ACT II

my failing immune system chokes my quality of
life with splotchy, sweaty palms. a firm,
controlling grip that i lack. i cannot even grip a
pen, and i am expected to get a grasp on my life?

ACT III

the staircase is a battle; every fucking day is a
war for survival. my greatest opponent is myself.
feverish chills, my veins are ice but my head is
somehow burning with an incurable fire. blood
pools in my feet, disanchoring my balance and
taunting the functionality of my loose limbs.

ACT IV

there is no rest for the wicked, no rest for this
disease. my bed is no longer a sanctuary of
peace, but midnight near-heart attacks where the
cage of my lungs can no longer control my
pulse. throat closes from the previous choke, a
cruel withholding of breath and unending ache.

ENCORE

each member of my body chants *more, more,
more* until i drown in my own diagnosis and
cannot crawl out from the depths of this disease

i. nostalgia is a slow, painful death. a disease that lingers, despite the photos you capture or despite how bloodied your fingernails become. from clawing at them to stay, for the moment to last just a second longer. you pick and preserve the flesh from beneath your crescent moon talons, yet it dies with a quiet ache. a pulsating whisper, a spiraling ebb that returns years later in a wave of deja vu.

ii. covid stole the thrill of growing up, my stagnant mind not evolving past sixteen. i would rather dwell in the comfort of the past, the fear of change is devouring me whole. swallowing each memory and chasing it with a shot of vodka, choking on empty promises to exchange letters or catch up over coffee. the aloneness consumes my anatomy, each vessel deteriorating. hanging on with a bittersweet shred of hope that time will slow down and things will last forever.

iii. i snip my bangs with my mother's sewing scissors, watching the strands melt into the bathroom linoleum as they fall. how ironic that i strive to change my appearance but fear the changing of my own life. i listen to joan dideon's *on keeping a notebook*, craving to preserve my youth in ink pens and poetry. but each word i write drowns with the last sunset of july, consumed by the mosaic mystery of the future.

THE RUIN OF IT ALL

i fear i am relationally ruined
eternally doomed, i advise you
to run before my words
dissolve your ego with acid.

i speak without thinking,
then think and dwell
and spiral without speaking

subject to silence
a million apologies
and insults
and curses
yet nothing
escapes my pale lips

my head feels
like paint drying
      slowly,   never   ending
a lazy river on fire
with no exit route
nor escape plan

i am overflowing
with rot and ruin
just a numb excuse
a waste of existence

i detest the words i speak
and regret the words i never spoke
and the thoughts i cannot dissolve
becoming more potent with time
the toxicity has taken over

there aren't enough metaphors
to describe the turmoil of my mind
i find myself content in the chaos
comfort in the lack of control

my mind is stagnant
water

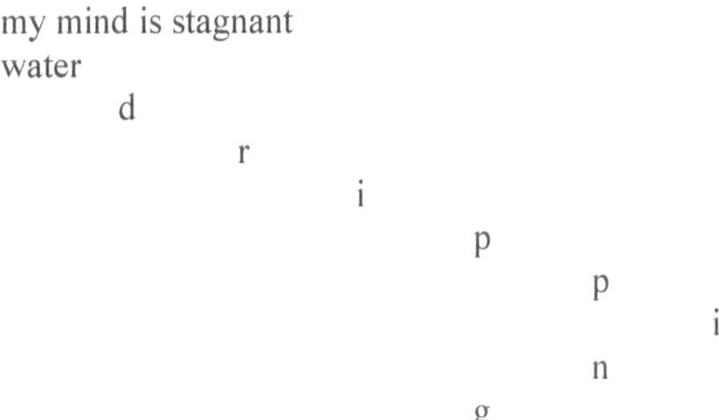

from a faucet
algae growing
of eclipse venom

i lock myself away so i don't
say the wrong thing and ruin
something or someone again,
so i cannot hurt anyone except for myself.
the tar on my hands, the leaky venom on my lips.
the poison consumes. burns.

i once broke

my bones
        to conform
                to submit
                        to squeeze
into the [mold]

until my surface   c r a c k e d
        i no longer feel a thing

and now

i am a shell
a vessel
starved of life

an [empty tomb]
an [abandoned home]

i   float
through my life

drifting across timelines
        lightly
                disconnected
from my obligations
        letting   go

HALF EMPTY /
A PIECE ON
TRICHOTILLOMANIA

my obsessive ritual,
a cyclical satisfaction-
yet here i sit, half bald
and half empty. are
you satisfied yet?

ripping each petal from
the garden of my scalp,
each follicle chanting
miserably until my ears
ring bloody silence, but
only temporarily.

a burning itch always
returns, a scratch that
can never satisfy until
every last hair is torn.

twisting the roots around
my tongue and swallowing
my pride, my dignity is
depleted into an ache.

MY SPIRIT WAS LOST IN THE WOODS WHEN I WAS TWELVE AND ALL THAT SURVIVED WAS MY BODY

i turned feral with a bleeding
shame between my legs,
all because eve was hungry,
starved for knowledge.

yet i also would rather
be haunted by reality than
naïve, a life is better lived
with a pulse than in hiding.

my girlhood reeks of mildew
chewed but never swallowed
instead spat for the greed
of the vultures and crows

to them i am just a body,
a submissive womb, an
emotional shotgun- loaded
but silenced.

my confirmation name is
disgrace, with a bruised
childlike faith and hoof
prints in the mud from
fleeing the predestined cycle.

she still remains somewhere
within the trees, lurking,
safe from all but the beady eyes
and spirits of the sacrificial lambs.

I GREENED OUT AND SAW GOD

i vomit colors of the communion
the bread, the body, the substance
the grape juice, mistaken for wine
my innocence is
            buried deep   within
me still, under   l a y e r s   of dirt and shame
skin *peeled* to reveal that
i remain soulless. i exist, i breathe
but do i truly live? my veins are
<u>rooted</u> in this body of stone,
barely functioning. praying,
the first time in months. are those
beliefs still deep down there
somewhere, in the abyss of my body?
i manually breathe and can't
remember how body knew, before.
she keeps me alive, keeps me well
so why do i destroy her?
i gain a new consciousness,
reincarnate as a sub-schizophrenic
body with a   disconnect   from the
earth below me and the hell that lies
beneath the blood **pooling** in my feet.
if i had perished, in my third story apartment
where would my final resting place be?
is there something worth believing
in this fleeting life, that determines
my future flourish or eternal torment?

I'D RATHER BE DRUNK

wasted tequila dripping
          down my journal
spilt ink and tears staining the pages
a constant hangover
but from the toxins of my own mind
i am mixed with >>> mayhem <<<
drawn to the {chaos}
agave nectar bleeds between the lines
sticky confessions ~~scratched out~~
a desire to live burns in my lungs
a strive to be mentally present
instead of just physically surviving
i'd rather be drunk, asleep
floating on the surface
not dead, just   gone
for a   while

WHEN I PERISH

i'll never be the chosen one
the wife, the prodigy, the one.
only a placeholder, a bookmark.
a temporary, compliant
fragment of the past

the prototype,
cloned and warped
then discarded
forgotten

gravestone carved
with my own nails

"here lies the woman
         who waited"

~~the wife, the mother~~
the placeholder.

CROWN OF THORNY NOSTALGIA

when i was eighteen and naïve
i wore a crown of summer's
eve flowers, weaved with
trust, ache, hope

i scorched my own bones
for them to notice me
set flame to my reputation
a burning bush of flesh

now i wear a crown of thorns,
of barbed wire. rust seeping
into my skull, bleeding
the fountain of youth

nostalgia has warped
my vision of the future,
i can't imagine myself
living past thirty

am i addicted to you
or is it just the nostalgia?
bonded by the tinted windows
of trauma, blinded by the buzz

knitting temporary
satisfaction through
my lonely ache, crafting
dust from my ribs
into diluted memories

GUILT FOLLOWS ME
LIKE A SHADOW

with   silent,   slithering
but evident footsteps
          lingering,   *looming*

this feeling of being
caught, shackled.
my feet are bruised,
calloused from running
from my own reflection

the townspeople scratch on
my bedroom door, claws
gripping flashlights and
pitchforks. an outsider to be tried
and hung, burned at the
stake of my own mistakes

i've wasted my whole life
hiding, scared to look back
at who may be following,
keeping tabs on my flaws
waiting to use it against me

i hide behind a mask of deceit,
life consumed by lies
i don't even know who i am
          i   never   have

MEMO: THINGS I'VE LOST
SUBJECT: MY RELIGION

the moment i knew that my faith was fading was when i was thirteen and i met a girl named hope. i always told myself that i didn't like girls the way that i liked boys, i just thought that they were pretty and soft, delicate. maybe it was gender envy, *i didn't want to be with her, i just wanted to be her.* when i was nine, i asked a girl when her breasts grew. i was so fascinated with a woman's body because i was so ashamed of my own, because i had nothing other than mosquito bites on a flat wooden board, with deepening splinters of envy growing into my heart. hope told me that she liked me on a crisp winter afternoon at the end of 2017, on a sunday. the lord's day. i remember the acid devouring the emptiness within my stomach. i withered under those words, face flushed with guilt and excitement of this forbidden newness. why was this crippling feeling, *love*, (or so i thought was love), a sin? i hope that if loving someone was a sin, the wrongness would be overlooked and god would accept that this is how he made me, with a spiritual connection beyond a physical body that just so happened to be cursed with a vagina. was it my fault that *fate* interfered from birth and gave me two x chromosomes and uncontrollable feelings for pretty girls. allegedly, everyone has a sinful nature, but *wasn't i born this way?* i hate labels, i just want to *feel* without criticism for human desire and experience. if i am shamed and unaccepted for simply loving someone, i will accept that i am a nasty sinner with the taste of rebellion on my tongue and an eternal curse for passion in which i cannot suppress or control.

MY MOTHER'S FAVORITE DISHES
S H A T T E R E D   ON THE CARPET
OF MY CHILDHOOD DREAMS

(disappointed)
about who i became
that my desires are different
than hers. the people pleaser in me
the eldest daughter
with a dandelion wish
to   carry   on the family
name, the sacred bloodline
by writing books instead of ~~babies~~

~~i'm sorry i'm sorry i'm sorry~~
you only know me through
this perception, this display,
this warped performance.
~~i've tried i've tried i've tried.~~
my best artwork, paraded
around the fairgrounds
begging for first prize,
while my bedroom carpet
is a hoarded sanctuary
of crumpled canvases
and broken dreams.
a palace of negligence
an infestation of
(disappointment)

MY GRIEF FOR YOU
RETURNS AS THE TIDE

you always crawl back when
i'm doing well. claw marks
on my calves from standing on solid
ground, above you on the quicksand. pulling
you further within your own delusion.
i was finally free from your grasp,
over it, over you. until
your false
contentment washes
away, the stinging saltwater of reality
burns your eyes. suddenly the appeal
of my success and what you had
haunts you. disturbing the
peace of my silent
waters, washing
up old letters
in bottles and memories
that had been untouched for so
long that crustaceans began to mistake
it for a shell, a home. i soon
remember the home
that i once had in you, the portal of surface
light that protected me from the depths
of my own, dark soul. you used me,
as a male anglerfish, a parasitic, pathetic
leech that lacks luminosity.
feeding on my own
light until you are recharged in order
to leave me again. and again.
and my grief returns.
again.

THIS WEED FEELS LIKE WHEN
I LEARNED ABOUT PREDESTINATION

the smoke in my lungs *s p i r a l s* into a psychosis, nails
grazing the pulse of subconscious rituals and ideologies
that were **nailed** into me since birth, as christ on the
wooden cross. he died for my sins, but did he want to?

was he predestined by god to fulfill his own created
prophecy? jesus sweat drops of bloody fear, begging his
father to take this cup of suffering. why was *he* chosen to
be the mediator, to obey the will of his designer? fully
flesh and bone, fully spirit, fully divine, fully
predestined to be the saving grace of a species
that was created to love him   unconditionally.
but then, is the love of god   conditional?

i remain captive under earthy layers of doubt, stuck
nailed to my own splintering board with the iron of
paranoia. watching my life go by and wondering if my
religious upbringing will ever cease to haunt my
existence, silently narrating with guilt, shame,
a desire to be holy.

if my destination is unchangeable, does anything matter?
the temple of my body that i **claw** at but will never
escape, predetermined by a divinely being-
so   distant it's almost   fictional.

THE DESENSITIZATION OF
AN EMPATHETIC HUMANITY

(BUT WAS HUMANITY EVER
EMPATHETIC?)

america forces blinders
on the eyes of the ignorant
a romanticized display of
      the false american dream
         that many would claw to have

but how can i ignore the screams
of innocent palestinian children,
      limbs lining the streets of rubble
we are disgustingly desensitized
with media normalizing blood
and bombings, just another scroll
another sunday swipe,   eyes glossed
over while a human life ends

while we cheer for the fireworks
that terrorize the veterans and the strays
and fuel the pockets of capitalism
the bombs trample neighborhoods,
                    blood of humanity splattering
                            the remains
my taxes fuel victory tweets
and greedy, greedy men in high,
unachievable places.

the rich line their pockets with
the   calloused   skin of
            underpaid workers
and the poor are pinching pennies
like   seagulls hoarding
            breadcrumbs
but greta thunburg is just
"an angry woman," right?
to invoke change,
            we need more
            angry women.

free palestine
free sudan
free congo
and all other
oppressed peoples.
no one is free
until we are all
free.

i suppose that i do bottle things inside of my fragile shell of a mind, as my self-preservative need for protection has hardened my heart within a tough casing.

my dad once said that he never saw me shed a single tear when my childhood dogs passed away. i often preached to my younger sister about holding everything inside, to not let her emotions show the vulnerability of weakness.

i haven't spilled the ooze of my mundane life into diary entries for years. *perhaps i have a fear of being found out, discovered- my dirty secrets revealed and analyzed, shattered with an ice pick and used against me in whatever punishment i am sentenced to, after they find out my gruesome, intrusive thoughts.*

i factually am aware that i'm not guilty, but my subconscious screams that i am a criminal, unworthy of human rights or happiness or anger or sadness. if they read my words, i am found out...

for loving and lusting and hating and wishing and longing, they may lock me in an asylum, which might be better off than the asylum of my own mind. *i often feel trapped as my thoughts spiral, with a nauseating sense of impending doom and unfiltered conscious.*

here i ponder, *with an uneasy rawness in my brain, of rotting psychological warfare.* barefoot beneath quilted roses and sheets of ivory in my childhood home, in my sister's old room. *the peeling walls of charcoal paint linger, sick with memories as i sit in diseased melancholy.*

the draft air and cyclical whirr of the box fan, *i can sense the metaphorical mold growth in my frontal lobe* as i type… delete… type… misspell… fuck… type and think and think and then bite my already short nails… wondering if there is an accumulation of fingernails in my empty stomach, conversing with earlier's oat milk espresso.

I NEVER HAD THE STARRING ROLE

a permanent understudy
to a perfect star, this   unreachable
idea of who i am supposed to be.
a   w a r p e d,   unrealistic   entity
that i worship, while shattering
the core of who i truly am.

i will never be the first choice.
how could anyone   choose me
if i cannot even   choose myself?

i cannot help that
i am obsessed with
perfection, it has been
nailed into me since birth.
society has told women
          what they are,   who they are
who   they should   be.

forever drooling, gnawing
at the the bars, [confined]
to the cell of my own
body, my eternal cage.

blindly grasping onto
the shred of hope until
my grip goes numb.
a rag doll, a limp zombie
of a broken girl consumed
by her own self loathing.

WHAT COLOR IS RAGE

a. the hole in my wall
b. the first time i was
       aware of my body
c. eternal punishment
       because of eve's naivety
d. my throat
e. biting the hand
       of god
f. hunger

the fruits of her bittersweet sadness, left to rot

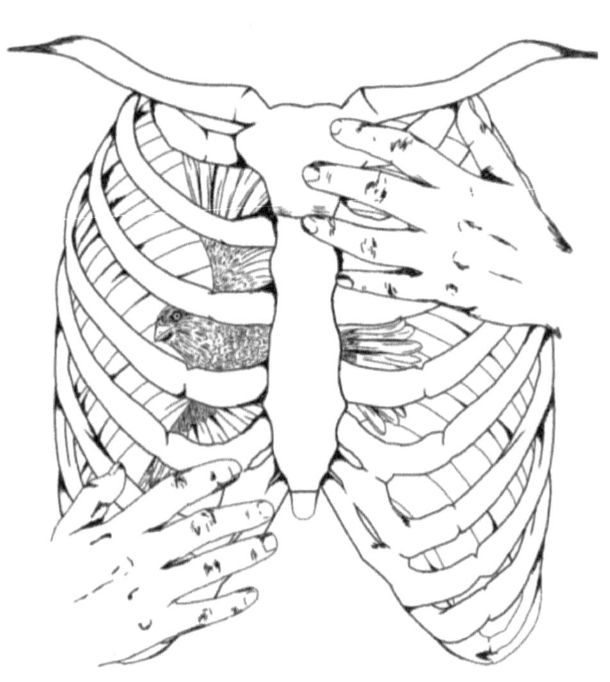

HUNGER

THE RIBS OF MY CARNIVOROUS
HEART ARE SHOWING

you are a

     sTiCkY

midwestern   summer,
     i am that { itch }
     you can never fully
     ~~scratch away.~~

a mosquito,   l i n g e r i n g
     in the humidity and <u>starved</u> of you.

i cannot help that i am an **ephemeral** pest,
     doomed   from the moment
     i hatched.   loving you is worth

the risk of being <u>crushed for my crave.</u> i am   < stuck >

in a   l o o p   of   ….. slowly…..   dying,
     asleep until i feel your gaze and suddenly my
clenched jawbone !!! C R A C K S !!! starlight
gleaming from my cavities. i am as **alive** as a nebraska
sunset,   … fading but briefly *euphoric*.

THE DECAYING CORPSE OF
A WOMAN ONCE CAPABLE OF LOVE

shriveled veins, dehydrated
from the bloodbath of fighting
for you. the sacrifices i've made
to defend your cruelty- humiliated
at how i just took it. over and over.
the smell of bleach, killing every
virus in my life but you. i am still
sick from gnawing at the leftovers
of us, the remains of my tenderness.
the rusted barbed wire of your voice
lingers, embedded in my side.

thorns tangled amidst my ribs, suffering
in the name of keeping you safe as
i slowly destroyed myself.
i am but a leech, attached to the idea of
who you were, but detached
from reality. an inability to move
forward. i willingly drown from
murky creek water in my lungs,
stuck in the mud. our roots were
buried deep, and i will die
with them. never to love again.

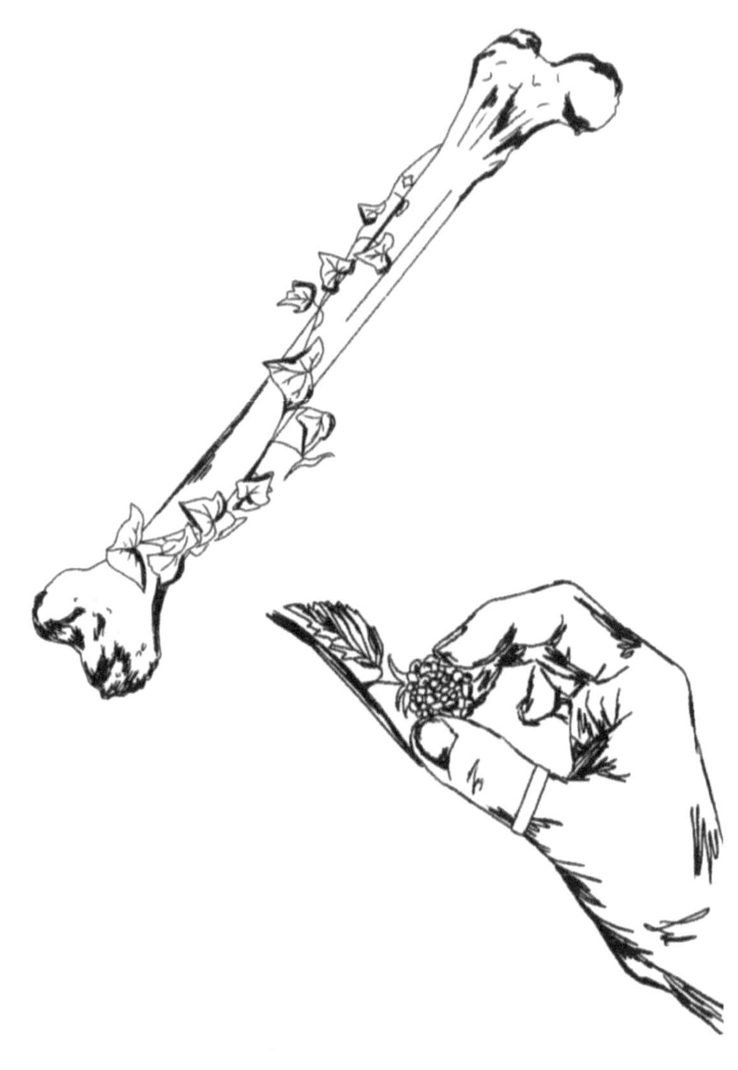

MY MUSE IN YOUR MARROW

you left your bones
behind on purpose,
for me to find. to treasure,
to adore and protect each part
of you in your absence.
i'll wash the fragments
with a bar of sensitive
ivory soap and soak them in
blackberry juice, framing
them in lace and longing.
i worship you. i'd allow you
to reach your fingers in
and graze my brain, praying
to the poetry that lives inside
of me. you'll find that you
are my muse. i'll wait by
my window until your return,
cradling your ligaments
and collecting dust until you
crawl back home to me.

A CAGED JACKALOPE

i have grown antlers, piercing
through my mythical skull
as bloodied claws, reaching.

you crave the hunt,
i dwell on an untouchable
pedestal and you want me.
not to nurture, but to own-
a zoo animal, taxidermied
proof of your power over me.

you have snipped my
emerging bones, plucked
my feathers and left me
barren of who i once was,
once overflowing with life.

your gaze is eerily like my
own, i see my fearful reflection
in your widened pupils. we are
the same, sins and all- except
i am the one caged. a prize.

I COLLECT FRAGMENTS OF YOU
AS AN OBSESSED CROW

the womanly desire to gather, foraging pieces of you that
were left for me to uncover. a cruel, deranged scavenger
hunt, knowing that this is the closest that i will ever get
to you. haunted by the drunk words and prolonged
glances, dangling it above my head. the comical torture
of my reaching, clawing. you are skin under my nails.
the alternate life we could have had, a perfect snow
globe nativity scene smashed into shards of reality,
to preserve what we will never have.

i can never be what you need. instead, i linger on the
unspoken. you'll never know the turmoil that boils
beneath the surface of my mind. the crave of the
forbidden apple- just a taste, a fantasy of a touch is more
appealing than who i really am, as opposed to who you
want me to be, to reflect your desires. this fictional
reality in which our reveries dictate, though unattainable.

you seek to maintain your own fire with more fire.
the burn within me does not possess the oxygen- the
answers you crave. instead, we should build a protective
shield around our minds, to limit the spark and kill the
reckless. i linger in suppressed thoughts.
i can't possibly name you, write it into existence because
then it could be found. seen. if i write it, i give it lungs.
a guilty pulse, a chance to be alive.

MY BURNING BONES,
BORN AGAIN

i have been petrified into
atheism and always felt
distant from the divine,
but there's something so holy
in your dark eyes that i might
believe just to spend eternity
worshiping each sin that lives
inside of your calluses.
my religion is in your
fingerprint, i mistake
my hell for heaven with
you beside my quivering
frame- even when you
are the one engulfing
my earthly vessel in flames.
my rotting heart is burning
alive again, born again.
i forgive you, i forgive it all.

LIKE A SPLINTER,
MY BODY REJECTS YOU,
DESPITE MY DESIRE

my want for you is
a burning itch, longing
to escape the cell of
my own flesh- chained,
contained. you are dead
to me, but i have
a need to crawl
into your grave
with you.

who is this corpse that
they call by your name?
i ate any evidence of
you alive in my life,
tormenting each vein
in my unforgiving body.

picking at the scab of us,
taunting me to sacrifice
my morals in order to
feel you bleed when your
absence makes me numb.

the cyclical ritual of hating
your guts and then singing
in the choir of obsession,
chanting your hymns that
ignite my insides alive.

LET ME BE YOUR LIGHTER FLUID

the x-ray / of my rib cage / reveals /
silhouettes of you. / skin crawling /
with forbidden desire, / my jaw
/ is slowly / c r a c k i n g / with guilt.
 / beneath the rotting / moss
/ ruins / of my masochistic soul, /
i can feel your toxins. / i am perfectly aware
/ that you / are the worst kind / of
poison / to me. / splintering nettles /
growing / in my lungs- / all i want /
to breathe / is you, / even if i choke. /
even if you / are smoke / to me. /
carbon monoxide. / i'd allow you /
to use me / as your ashtray, / brand
my skin / like a cowboy / to his /
beloved cattle. / douse / my spark, /
just to ignite / your own. / [to own
me] / just let me / i'd let you /

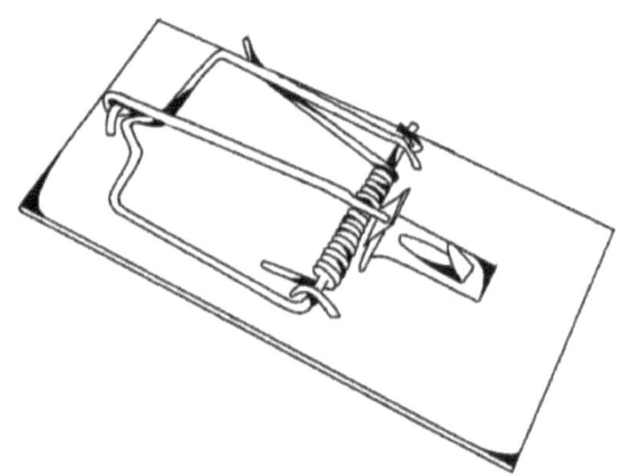

MY EMPATHY HAS BEEN BEATEN
INTO A CURSE.

my scarlet summer
nights faded, soon painted
with your bruised blue. how
quickly i forgave when
purple was all i knew.

you plucked my naïve
feathers and left me barren,
kindness stripped
from my soul.
i don't trust anyone
after you punished
my blind faith.

my stomach is full of orange peels
your acidity clings to my insides
no matter how many fingers
i shove down my throat
to vomit the rotten love
you quickly made
a mockery of.

I UNDERSTAND THE ZOMBIES NOW
ALL I CRAVE IS YOUR BRAIN

you weave fraying threads of
mystery underneath the crevices
of my dismantled brain. i have an
inner turmoil of never knowing who you
truly are. it haunts my withered, aching core

i beg, write me a novel
let me dissect your mind
analyze the puzzles of poems
interpret the unspoken
allow me to understand you
if you'd just let me in

i will peel away my pride and
intertwine within your spine
the invasive vines of my devotion
growing between your evergreen veins
rooting deep within your subconscious

anchoring, claiming.
tenderly crocheting the
spiderwebs that dwell
in the vacant home that
you built for our secrets-
abandoned, waiting for
this storm to cease

I'M YOUR DAISY [EDGAR]
JONES [& THE SIX]

 - YOU REGRET ME
AND YOU WON'T FORGET ME

two halves of the same rotten,
infested apple- molded with stolen
glances and longing. universally
untouchable and doomed from
the beginning. fucked up, destined to fail.
still, i write the same three damn
poems and they are all about you.

perhaps i am a fictional fantasy of
a character you know so well; broken
bones, a shattered soul that mirrors
your own. you are nicotine, caffeine-
bringing out the worst but so addicting,
intoxicating. i hate that i see myself in you.

our flaming souls were crafted with
the same fiber; magnetic, maddening.
so holy, our forces fight like a tornado
and a hurricane- together we
make a disaster with no solidity to depend on.
you were never supposed to be
my soulmate, but a twin flame.
you taught me how to burn, a passion
within myself that needed a spark to
ignite my potential. to soar, without you.

THE   HOLE
IN MY COLD HEART

there is a ripening ache
that is shaped like you
within my ribs, i have
lost any faith of healing
from this blistering bruise.
a sliver of my soul will
always need you, that
will remain tender
and raw until i am
six feet within the dirt.
even then, the beetles
and the fungi will only
taste your name within
my fading muscle tissue.
the only fragment of me
with any life remaining
is the part that remembers
you. i will decompose
with those rotten memories,
still as alive as how you
once made me.

SHADOW PUPPETS

i am the rabbit, you are the dog
      chasing >>> me through my ~~dreams~~
torturing them into <u>nightmares</u>

i am   never   fast enough to
escape you, even if i
spend my entire life
breathless, running

your holographic memory
is ***branded*** within my skull,
shadows plastered on my wall
despite the bleach that b l i s t e r s
my palms from SCRUBBING ~~away~~

i'd rather be an insomniac than
have to ~~hide~~ for eternity,
my bed has become a   [**pit**]
of despair as you wait
patiently with mouth agape
and claws prepared for a feast.

i'm done allowing your
bony fingers to control me,
i am your sock puppet no more.
my bloodshot eyes are the
emblem to my new kingdom,
and now you must starve.

AM I FORGETTABLE,
LIKE FREEZER BURNT MEAT

my plastic mask, a disguise.
painting my face, engraved.
prepared to be *used*
swallowed then spat
my edges are moldy from
        MoRpHiNg
my desirability slowly decaying
shoved to the depths of
my mother's garage freezer
a museum of preserved potential,
dated and labeled and saved.
        but the perfect moment for
        my debut will never come
i am otherworldly, never
meant to be devoured
instead lingering on the
past and growing   *cold*

FRANKEN-BRIDE

how can you forget
about me if you keep
creating my clone?

you hang her
on the wooden cross
above your door,
but you know that
she can never
save you from
yourself.

she morphed into an
entity with your twisted
idea of perfection,
because i broke free
from the reins that you
carved into my
spiteful tongue.

i was made to be
more than yours
and you hated that.
those lustful, wire fingers
can no longer stitch my
venomous lips together.
you detested your lack
of control, that i was more
than a suburban mother,
a submissive wife.
i am a threat to your empire,
and you fear my bite.

DISPLAYED LIKE A DEAD FISH ON

A WHITE BOY'S FACEBOOK POST

you strum
the strings
of my heart,
stripping
the melody
and leaving
me barren

each gaze
          pulls me in
on your strings
in a fishing line
tangled
within your
mess

taunting me,
holding
our future
above my
head

and then trampling
any remnants
of hope, stabbing
my back with
the shards of
my broken
dreams

SOBER AVOIDANCE
DRUNK TRUTH

you **need** me and it
fucking terrifies you.
no matter how cold
you treat me, no matter
where you run to, you
can never hide from
your subconscious

although you lock
me out of your mind
and swallow the key,
the secrets overflow
when the liquor hits
your veins, and suddenly
every vessel cries for me

a moth to my flame
of burning embers,
a magnetizing grasp.
so   distant but so
inescapable

does the high
blur my reality
or **magnify** the truth
for you?

I THOUGHT I WAS JUST
A TEMPORARY MUSE,
AND A TERRIBLE LOVER

but he loves me with my unshaven legs
and worships my frizzy hair.
to him, my morning coffee breath
and aphrodite the stomach
are the sexiest things ever

my mouth full of "fucks" and
leftover eyeliner, smudged
down my freckled cheekbones,
my dirty depression hoodies
and the dishes i keep ignoring,
hoping they just disappear

when i make him my monkey
and i am the amateur esthetician,
or when i cut my bangs and dye them
~~red black blonde green blue black brown~~
~~black brown~~ black. he even loves me when
when the green peeks through, or
when i jab metal into my lip to feel pretty.

my flat ass in those mom jeans
and when the amaretto makes
my laugh evolve into a wheezing snort.
he still looks at me with the same
gentle eyes, even if i changed myself
completely from sixteen, eighteen, twenty-one.

there is a bittersweet intimacy / in knowing
/ that i will never / speak to you again /
the aching / watercolor grey / of my iris /
will never / again / hold / your fading gaze
/ and somehow / knowing that / makes
me treasure / our blurred moments / more

and i wonder / if my scent / will haunt you /
the floral vanilla / infused within my hair /
i hope you've forgotten / how to breathe /
lungs choking / on the smoke / of the words
i wrote / about you / how i still see you /
in the eyes / of ghosts, / lovers, / strangers.

the fruits of her bittersweet sadness, left to rot

the fruits of her bittersweet sadness, left to rot

the fruits of her bittersweet sadness, left to rot

EARTH

EVERY MEMBRANE
CONNECTS ME TO MY
MOTHER EARTH

my neon veins branch out, reaching
like the limbs of ancient oak trees
and stretched to glorify the handmade
heavens. each lighting strike, every
vessel, an intentional detail of
history intertwined.

the fibonacci sequence-
each spiral mirroring
the crevices of my fingerprints
or the intricacies of
a twisted seashell. a fossil
reflecting each ocean wave,
tree stump, galaxy, hurricane,
tentacle, cochlea or embryo.
each curve, i pray reverently
to the silent wonder of it all.

we are one with the natural world,
humanity is of no greater importance
than the limitless of our earth.
we are never truly alone, forever
dwelling under the stars of
possibility and connection to
something much larger
than our own lives.

IF I WAS A PERFUME, AS AN ANXIOUS POET

<u>top notes:</u> sage / manic pixie dream girl essence /
raw vanilla / sprig of lavender / consciousness
of being alive / incense and smoke / brain fog /
torn skin on my fingertips / that house in nebraska /
shitty latte art / desire to be everything but nothing/
to stand out but blend in

<u>middle notes:</u> the blood of pomegranates / clippings
of moth wings / antlered roadkill on the gravel /
loose leaf tea / a rusted hatchet / disassociation /
blackberry /male manipulator music / parentified
english professor /the morning after a thunderstorm
/ stagnant attic air

<u>base notes:</u> the fig tree analogy / constant sense
of impending doom / prairie grass / woodland moss
/ shards of glass / waves of intense derealization /
the girl, interrupted film / identity crisis / magnolia
petals / flesh / the end of radiohead's "let down"

PURE INTENTION OF
PEELING A FRUIT

the precious peel,
a journey of sticky fingertips
through layers of complexity
to reach the core, a fountain
of blissful juice waiting
to honor your tastebuds.

versus the frozen fruit, the easy
route with a reward of shriveled,
depleted nutrients. destined
to de-thaw instead of dripping
bloody ripeness.

the raw, authenticity of
a sunset dripping mango
after you slice her surface,
an unpeeled tangerine,
waiting for the one
to gift her goodness.

most wouldn't linger
to get their hands sticky
in order to digest each layer
of me, unknown of the treasure
i savor for whoever has the patience
to handle my swollen soul
before it rots.

METAMORPHOSIS

perhaps humans were never intended to know who we were meant to be, the same way we were never intended to see our own reflection except for in murky puddles, emerald lakes, eyes of lovers. i am just a scrapbook of idols, a vessel of admiration. *my bones worship the creators, the artists, the designers.* a desire to morph into different versions of myself, to reinvent, to mimic- molding my brain like clay. i've spent my entire existence searching for the meaning of it all, discovered that my soul was crafted from the same fibers as the roots of a weeping willow. my own roots reach so deeply that they *graze the graves of ancient poets, burnt witches* and backyard burials of lifeless sidewalk birds. i pick shards of each memory from the canals of my admiring heart. *i am but a vessel of tribute* to the immortal arts of this fleeting life, soul outliving my body by reflecting the everlasting words within my being.

THE MUSHROOMS MADE YOUR
PUPILS LOOK LIKE COSMIC SINKHOLES

our goosebump bitten legs / sink into the leather couch /
minds melting within the meaning of it all / with a slight
ache / of impending doom / our hollow eyes meet and /
my pulsating heart thuds / so fiercely that i can feel / my
rib cage crack / as the walls whisper / secrets to my
psyche. / the disconnect   of my body / from my
soul / is spiritual, / acid tears burn my cheekbones / as i
pray / to whatever god i feel / so fiercely in this moment
/ maybe someday i'll know them. / my old self was left
behind / that night, / but i do not mourn. / her bones are
safe, / buried in an empty cornfield, / with ashes
scattered amongst / the gravel of my nostalgia.

SPITTING THE BUTTERFLY WING
DUST FROM MY TASTEBUDS

an arachnid, i have eight limbs
all reaching in opposite directions,
pulling the threading of my
muscles apart towards each
aspect of potential in my life

i possess a fervent desire to be
everywhere, be everyone.
to become one with the universe-
to melt within the magma casing
of the earth's core. every day
of my life is a performance

my insides are hollow, stomach walls
stretched, bruised by the constant need
to consume: media, opinions,
jagged fingernails, conformity.

a need to return to my roots,
to who i am. the twisted vines and veins
in my eyes, to release the fluttering
sparrows from my ribcage. swallowing
songbirds and coughing up feathers,
i choke on my words and metaphors
no one understands, no one even tries

spitting the butterfly wing dust from
my tastebuds and plucking the loud people
from between my teeth. to freely trace
the constellations etched on my spine,
the true embroidered colors of my soul.

THE COMFORT OF TORNADO
SEASON IN THE MIDWEST

midwesterners can "smell" the rain, clouds of murky ash
rolling across the plains. cattle waltzing home before the
dust consumes the valley, cornfields and power lines
swaying in preparation. i stand on the porch with my
hands on my hips like my father, with his handkerchief
in one pocket and a knife in the other. radio static that
crunches like leaves beneath my boots with the national
service weather man on the hand crank receiver.
he greets me like an old family friend, voice eerie
yet so familiar. the wind whispers like a
coyote howl, a distant warning. springtime
in tornado alley brings a peace only
understood by few. a connection built
on the limestone foundation of
generational bonds, trust in my
grandmother's creaky wooden
porch. amateur storm
watchers, capturing
grainy photography
and risky memories
to return with
each new
storm
cell.

SAFE IN THE ARMS OF MY DAD'S BUICK

westbound on highway 128,
toward the setting sun, with
a gas station coke and
heavy eyelids, fluttering.
drifting asleep in the rear of my
dad's old car, the blues and
nirvana on the stereo as my lullaby.
my adult life in the city seems
so far away when i am protected
by the radio static of local stations.

distant farm trucks breathe
gravel and exhale dust clouds,
specks that i can pinch between
my fingertips like tiny ants
with wheels. sun rays casting
shadows on windmills and
abandoned barns, hills of
cornfields and dreams of
childhood, a safe haven
in the back of that buick.

an uprooted tree on the hill
waves to me, her veiny limbs
admiring the glimpses of
lilac and lavender in the clouds.
i dream that i can admire
my midwest forever through
childlike eyes, in the comfort
of those worn fabric seats.

HEALING MY MOON
BY LOVING THE SUN-
ECLIPSED

you taught me to worship my own
blemishes, the scars that define
my inward and outward entity.

your calloused, tender hands hold
me as i melt within the craters of
your otherworldly eclipse

the way our bed is our alter, crafting
love spells in the stillness of the night-
holy under the midnight glow of the moon

you cradle me within my grave
and illuminate who i was meant to be,
lighting the spark that set my heart on fire

the dried petals of our preserved laughter,
goosebumps and love notes kept in
glass jars to keep our memory alive.

you are my sun, golden pools of
eternal serenity. i wouldn't mind getting
sunburnt from the ultraviolet
light of your july rays

A COMPUTER CANNOT FEEL THEREFORE A COMPUTER SHOULD NOT CREATE

have you ever shot awake at 3 am, squinting reaching for a pen and a receipt scrap, jotting down a slice of a poem and misspelling the word marijuana??? creating galaxies on the pages and then ripping them out of your journal because the feelings were too intense for human eyes to see??? finding music in the veins of tree trunks, passion in the dim lights of a dive bar, magic in the eyes of your lover??? we have lost creativity, discarded the beauty of being MESSY!!!! destroying our planet for a deeply flawed, warped idea of perfection!!!!!

LICK THE HONEY
FROM MY LUNGS

be patient with me
my frozen heart is
like crystallized honey
waiting to be melted
as i learn to trust again
i de-thaw with the
warmth of your
gentle, tender embrace

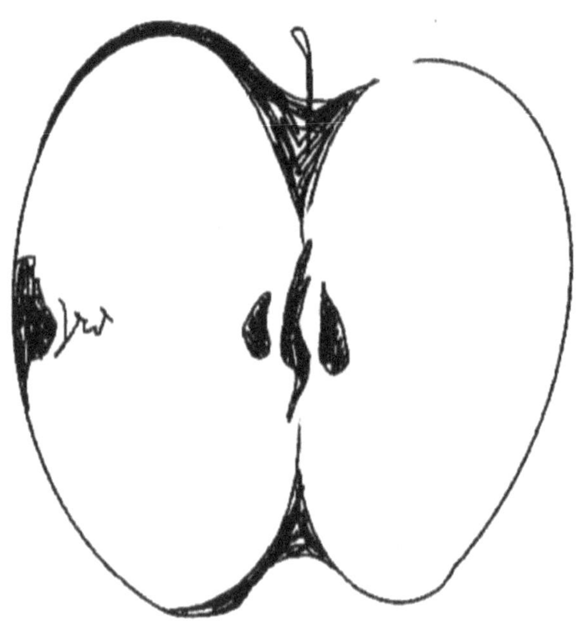

AN ODE TO EVE

my nakedness is not
inherently a sin,
the curse of my
womb, defined by
the apple of my
own eye. the
fruits of my labor,
a punishment for
human existence

oh, curious eve
calculated
by her own fate,
to be destined for
a life of blame
shamed for the *want*
of consciousness, to be
all knowing
to be at ease
instead of a life
of searching

is knowledge such a curse?
to have free will is to
clear the fog, autonomy.
the ease, freedom to just *know*
the mother of my pain,
she who paced barefoot
in the garden of doom-
i empathize

THE DEVIL & ANGEL ON MY SHOULDERS MEET FOR LUNCH

one swings from an invisible rope wrapped round my throat. the other, perched on my hoop earrings, voice raw and earthy, like my mother's. "we are both looking after her," says the angel, feathers angled upward. towards the stars, a glimpse of heaven. "well, i have her best interests in mind," replies the devil, teeth sharp and coated with blood and black tar. "she is full of worldly sentiment; lungs full of incense and smoke, skin marked with unnatural scars and permanent ink, stomach twisted with lust and overflowing with acidic wine. she is a reflection of your ungodly influence."

"get your teeth out of her, she only listens out of fear because of what you've nailed into her."
they both sit in silence. "i was always just trying to protect her." the divinely being pleads. "sometimes you need to take a step back and let her breathe, she won't be able to fly if she's never allowed to use her wings."
my guardian devil spits the last words like a fiery force.

the angel pauses, wings lowered as she takes a bite of the tangerine within her palm. juice as clear as rainwater flows from the core, river of silence between the two immortals. she contemplates for a moment, while the devil lights up a cigarette and blows the smoke into the face of the other. the angel turns the other way, facing the city, the world she is so afraid of.

"don't you think that we are both here for a purpose?" one asks the other. "to serve and protect, to oversee that this human's path aligns with her destiny and fulfills the will that is expected upon her, of course." the angel spits the seed of the fruit off of my shoulder, disappearing into dust below. maybe a stem will grow from it, roots reaching for the core of the earth.

"perhaps, but i am here to encourage mistakes, to be curious and brave. to experiment, to experience. there is a lesson to be learned in everything under the sun. the ugly, the forbidden, the evil, the rotten, the bitter, the sinful. there can be no growth without rain, no evidence of human existence without scars and bruises, death and life and rebirth and decay. i would rather have lived a full life than be dictated by fear."

the devil ashes the nicotine stick on my shoulder, becoming another freckle, or scar, or proof of my existence.

MY MOTHER'S BONES

the sharpness of my metacarpal
mirrors that of my mother's.
we share the same jawline
rounded, apple cheekbones-
bone structure hidden
beneath our softness

her gentle hands
folded, polite, praying
slender, tender fingers-
eternally busy. tasking,
preparing, serving without return

i catch myself mirroring her,
speaking through hand motions
expressive fingertips,
dancing in the air
like shadow puppets
singing me to sleep
memorizing the psalms

worn, torn, cracked
from dirty dish water
and nurturing her herbs
as if they were her own offspring,
ever since my sister and i grew up.

i hope that i mirror her inward,
as much as her outward.
that i am as soft, gentle as her
a servant heart that outflows
unconditional kindness.

INFINITE

the moonlight sheds a tear
on your brow bone,
eyes gleaming as the stars
kiss your hazel iris.
tracing my freckles
that the sun left as gifts,
you declare us infinite.
perks of being a wallflower
has always been my favorite
film; you have always seen
me for who i am. in all of my
rawness, not who i try to be.
not for who i perform as,
for the crowd to weep with laughter
or throw spoiled fruit at.
you read my soul and know me.
listening to the words of my heart,
even when i don't say a thing.

POETIC PERSPECTIVE OF "I" (EYE)

poets view the world through the same lens, we share the same shard of perspective that was harvested from a sliver of moonlight, her gift to her mortal servants. each fluorescent glow of her rays represents an unspoken connection to each other, to the universe, to the *melting* and *meshing* and *molting* of individuals and their ideas. does beginning a poem with "i" make me selfish? repetitive? monotonous? or does the flick of the "i" with the dotted tip leave space for self insertion, for readers to fill the gap with their own experiences and lives. my thoughts also belong to you, dear reader. to have and to hold, to *nurture* and *nourish* you. may we all find comfort, an unspoken understanding in the "i." to be seen, through the eyes of the hurting. though miles, lifetimes, decades, and lightyears separate our bodies, our minds will defy the bounds of science and *connect* through the spiritual realm of *creativity*.

NOSTALGIA WILL CONSUME ME,
MY VEINS REMAIN SIXTEEN

a blown-out stick and poke tattoo from my ex best friend
/ nameless yellow wildflowers that grow free on gravel
roads /a pandemic that drained the color from the world,
from me. /a sip of whiskey, throat coated in guilt / dyed
my hair cherry red, blotchy, but new. / i needed change /
the world as i knew it was fading away / time is still
frozen from when the world   paused /
i am forever sixteen. / smoking for the first time on the
graffitied playground / a burnt juul pod on the steps of
the methodist church / anything to rebel, to prove i was
alive / when the world seemed so dead / so empty, so
lifeless. / a proof of existing, a plea to live.

COLD, CRANBERRY DRIPPINGS

warm, sticky purple dances down my chin, dripping onto my fuchsia swimsuit. the popsicle stings the raw gaps of gum tissue from my missing baby teeth, yet the sweet acidity that lines my eight-year-old belly is worth it. criss cross applesauce on the clay patio tiles, the hot pavement burning my skin slightly from the warm june sunlight.

my sandy blonde curls are anointed with holy water from my grandmother's pool, forehead blessed with an imprint of my goggles. nana passes out more "juice-sickles" to my cousins and i, a traditional concoction within our small family. the flavor this afternoon is a mix of tangy cranberry and grape juice, a sour sensation that tickles our tastebuds.

tiny, wet footprints trail down the sidewalk to the humble, white house- likely from my baby cousin who could no longer hold her bladder. my younger sister's blonde locks are matted, but she couldn't care less. she caresses the family cat, dave, brushing his apricot-colored fur between her sticky popsicle fingers as he licks the drip from the pavement. he purrs, leaving his fur behind as a gift as he rubs against the condensation on my skin.

toothless smiles radiate across the yard; each childlike grin over-lined with messy popsicle lipstick. nana places a green plastic bowl in front of each of us, overflowing with sangria-colored grapes. her dark swimsuit reveals her hidden butterfly tattoo, i trace the faded colors with my bitten fingernails and imagine my own skin in the future, plastered with artwork to transform myself into a gallery of memories.

my grey eyes flutter closed, eyelashes still dripping with a hint of chlorine. i fall asleep, dreaming of sweet summertime. we would have five more summers left until my cousin's moved across the state, and they go from a daily part of my childhood routine to a scrapbook page, a text message every six months, a facebook post, a murmur of a memory.

MY SOUL OUTLIVES MY BONES

i want to be everyone and everything but also nothing. to be a known poetess, for my name to be listed among sylvia plath, virginia woolf, maya angelou, emily dickinson, mary oliver. i yearn to be extraordinary, but also ordinary. a rusted box of rotting letters and diaries, discovered by historians and displayed in a museum, as an anonymous woman living in the early twenty first century. a small, midwest community's best kept secret, my birthplace a hidden sanctuary for the migrating birds to dwell along their journey south. i am but a simple woman with an aching desire to blend in. to die with an unmarked grave in a forest cemetery, headstone overgrown with moss. the only flowers i receive are kisses by the morning dew, greeting my remains with the gentlest of touch. though the world moves forward with time's cruel reality, nature will never allow me to be forgotten. my legacy melts within the dark earth, my soul outliving my bones through my poetry.

THE DRAGONFLIES SWARM

above my frame,
as the blackened clouds weep.
a storm is brewing like bubbling tea
in the kettle. it's almost as if
the insects know something,
as if this world has become
so warped that they know
this isn't normal. they aren't
desensitized to tragedy
as america is. the thunderheads
seem to graze the bottom ozone
later, drifting towards the chaos.
as if each molecule within them
is being dragged down, as if
the lost lives on earth are connecting
the heavens to the human. the recent
lynchings, grotesque genocide,
cultural divide. hundreds of
dragonflies dance, but not
from joy. they preform a mourning
ritual, wings fluttering as a prayer
to the planet. a plea for compassion,
for empathy, for the return to our
roots. if only adam never emerged
from the dust. if only we had left
the garden untouched. the mortal
greed would cease to exist,
and the wildlife would
finally know peace.

/ i envision myself / twenty years from now, / newly formed creases live amongst my faded olive freckles. / late july kisses my sunspots as an old friend, / each smile line a representation / of the joy / that endlessly overflows / across my lifetime. / each silver strand / earned like medals, / crowing my head / with glory- / glimmering proof / that i've lived. / she tenderly holds / each memory / within the crevices of her palms, / the soul of that little freckled girl / still running freely, / leaving footprints scattered / like breadcrumbs / throughout the timelines. /

/ i blink, / feeling five years old again, / tugging on the trim / of my mother's denim skirt. / peering into the glass / windows downtown, / i steal a glance / from a young woman / on the other side. / she has my mother's sapphire eyes, / my mother's cocoa curls, / my mother's cheekbones and dimples. / i notice the same grey birthmark / on my forearm as her own, / a kiss / from our ancestors. / she is radiant, / she exemplifies the truest fragments / of me. / she is me. / i no longer fear / the gift of aging, / nor do i fear / becoming my mother. /
the invisible bond / between mother / and daughter / is interwoven / with complexity- / envy, / reflection, / expectations, / potential. / i embody / all she could've been, / and she is all / i can become. / what a beautiful, / inevitable / future. / no matter how far / i run / from my reality, / i will never escape / the beautiful blood / within my veins. /

SO CELESTIAL

sometimes i don't feel real / you
make me feel real / does everything
happen for a reason? / are we meant
to be in another universe? / i've never
been to the moon / but i've looked
into your eyes / and felt craters form
in my stomach / i'm not religious /
but i feel so celestial / so alive /
with your fingers intertwining
with my soul / you see me /for who
i am / not who i try to be /

a humid / midwestern summer /
muffled laughter / under the blood moon
/ wild mulberries / stain my fingertips /
wind in my hair, / still feeling seventeen
/ a missouri highway / leading to nowhere /
tonight smells like weed / with a trace of iowa
/ one of those moments / that you will
remember / forever

TO ME, YOU ARE THE LAST RAY
OF A MELTING SUNSET

a gleam of light follows you
around in tiny golden footsteps,
an invisible energy that is
warm and a breath of fresh air.
to me, you are freshly cut grass,
a sleepy sunday morning,
a blossoming field of wildflowers
in july- untouched to everyone
but the bumblebees
and deer.

you inspire me to keep treading
water, to keep coming up
for air despite my internal need
to drown quietly. you dive into
my silent soul and i begin to crave
the air, i long to uncover the hidden
secrets of the surface, the ones
i had been hiding from for so long.

you gently pull me out of my shell
and encourage me to sprout wings
and fly, feathers fluttering through
my beautiful life with you in the pastel
clouds, by my side. even if i soar
too out of control, you ground me
with consistency and support.
i begin to float downwards from
my spiral, fog lifted from my mind
for just a split second. i can touch
the petals of calmness, feeling
each leaf between my fingertips
and breathe- all because of you.

our love is unbreakable, a constant
flow even amidst the chaos of this
fading planet. such a unique connection
of two souls, a connection that only
drifts along every few decades or so.
i have never been as sure of a person
before you. you complete me- body,
soul, spirit. if everything else in my
life crumbles, i am content as long
as i have you. you are so full of good,
you are the definition of good.
you exemplify good, in all of
it's pureness and rawness and
glimmer.

HARVEST MOON

and suddenly, my complaints
seem so minuscule under a
new moon and a sky

d r i p
        p i
n g

with fragments of light.
there is a comfort knowing
that the stars remain the same,
despite how i change.

BATHED IN THE { HOLY
WATER } OF THE GALAXY TUB

i sweat purple beads
of blackberry juice,
mulberry stained fingertips
as the artificial coloring
disguises my auburn hair
into a greenish blue

mascara flakes softly kiss
my freckled cheekbones,
grazing each scar and
blemish as if they were
the most heavenly
glimpse of perfection

trying to morph the fleshy
canvas my soul was born within,
my avatar becoming more *me*
with every wrinkle, tattoo, and
metal caressing my skin

the purpose of my life isn't
to   *find myself,*
but to   *create myself-*
to // alter | the altar \\within
the [sacred temple]
of my vessel.

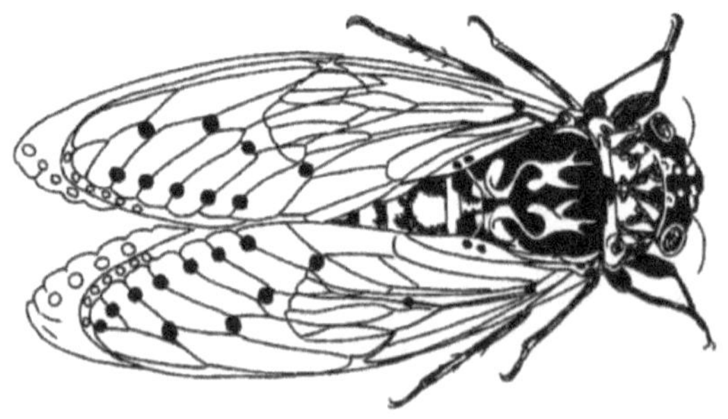

TO EVERY BEGINNING, AN END AWAITS

there is an acorn in the mulch, fallen from the mother oak tree that shadows over the siding of the brick house. the cicadas sing a dying, september melody, the distant chirps sound like summer's end- an expectancy of death and time passing with nothing you can do to stop it. the wind shushes the insects, leaves rustling like a midwestern ocean- waves fading in and out as the crickets hum a lullaby. everything feels so simple out here, with the breeze in my hair, like nothing else matters. the limbs of the oak grow deep and tall, moss caressing them at the base. i imagine their veiny roots reaching towards the magma within the core but they will never get there. likewise, they reach parallel towards the grey abyss, clouds circling. i can almost hear them chant, *a storm is coming,* yet they cannot escape. they do not run, because they thirst to maintain their green. but autumn will come regardless, and they will fade into brown, sprinkles of dust.

OUR EARTH WILL
SOON BE A GRAVEYARD

moss glazes over the headstones, forgotten to all but the ghosts and roly-polies. names now illegible, once so full of life, even in death. the tips of the trees are kissed with maroon lipstick, watercolor paintbrushes sprinkled along the graveled roads. a sign of autumn's beginning, but the year's end. the squirrels scatter like scattered glass as i draw closer, scurrying beneath the tree line and hidden from the light rain fall. even if my species goes extinct, our mother earth would still live on. would that be so tragic? skyscrapers overgrown by greenery, much like a worldwide malaysian forest city. i think of the biomimicry life's principles, how overgrown the national parks would become and how clean the air would be- free of smoke and chem trails. the flourishing of a society that returned to its roots, evolving and adapting without mortal limitations. how life was supposed to be lived, intended to thrive- even in death. each walking corpse today will someday become a bacterial feast, the end signifying a cycle of beginning.

I DETEST MY BODY UNTIL
I REMEMBER THAT I AM
NOT A TEMPLE, BUT A
WILDERNESS

the stretch marks creep along my bruised thighs like
morning glories, wild irises blossom within the garden
of my overgrown bikini line, remaining untamed. my
stomach spills over my buttoned jeans, a bubbling
brook- an altar for the nourishment that i am so
privileged to consume. there is something so sacred
about my imperfections, proof that i lived my life, and i
lived it well. i am the roots that reach deep into the clay
earth and graze the pits of hell, but i also am the auburn
branches that praise heaven with the wind. yes, i rot but i
also am reborn with each new season, i may decompose
but is that so bad? to become a feast for the starving
creatures, to re-enter the cycle through giving life to
another soul. i'm not scared of burial because i am
overflowing with dirt. i do not hunger to die anymore,
because death already seeps from my mouth;
but so does life.

the fruits of her bittersweet sadness, left to rot

EVERYTHING ROTTEN
MUST DECOMPOSE

EVEN YOUR MELANCHOLY
WILL SOMEDAY DISSOLVE

AND YOU WILL BE SET FREE

the fruits of her bittersweet sadness, left to rot

the fruits of her bittersweet sadness, left to rot

the fruits of her bittersweet sadness, left to rot

excerpts from leta iris's

debut poetry collection,

when summer fades to fall

my bones will forever be buried in nebraska

meet me by the old oak tree in the town i was born in,
between the veiny roots of age and beneath the dirt of
your worn fingernails. my feet are blistered with anxiety,
limbs bruised from the tread of fighting for survival. i
ache. lay with me until our bodies melt into the earth
and our bones merge over centuries of embrace.
the world as we know will soon fade away, you and i
remain. collect treasures from the graveyards of glass
underground, a garden of garbage buried by the ghosts
of neighbors before. maybe they left it for us to discover,
decades later. i'll cough up rusty nails and pick shards of
metal from your throat, saving them as proof of our
existence. we can rest here for a while, protected by the
heartland as the chaos of the world wastes away. until
then, the sun will set over my midwestern prairie for the
last time.

the space between

my mind is rotten with nostalgia,
with all of my creativity
swallowed up by my childhood.

i live in my head,
an unreliable narrator,
numb to reality.

raw honey seeping from my ears,
a beehive of inspiration,
pollinating the wildflowers of ideas
while i dismiss my own life.

i am unable to move forward,
stuck between the pages of the past-
fulfilling fantasies that one day
i will grow wings,
piercing through my spine
and lifting my uneasy thoughts away.

i ache to rest in the
      quiet
           between

memory   and   reality.

you are a cavity, a curse

floss my teeth with your hair,
split ends brittle from cruelty.
you have never been
tender, merciful.
deceased to me, a zombie of
lust that infects my brain and
controls my pulse.
rotten meat of your memory
lingers in my mouth,
stuck as am i.
watch the ivory bones
decay from the
sweetness of your toxins,
i remain addicted,
you remain a part of
my dna forever.

caffeine cravings

he felt like caffeine, only i am dead.
my heart of leather, i am too far gone.

the drug does nothing-
as persephone yearns to
greet me at the gates.

my blood stains the cutting board
as i open, pouring my words
into the ceramic bowl
and leaving me vulnerable.

an act of trust.
the desire of flesh-like
seeds drove him mad,
with the blade he held
mauling my core.

my worth is measured by
how easily i am tamed,
how i serve.

ribs stitched together
with a singular vine of ivy
in an attempt to revive me,
but i am too far gone
into my insanity.

even after death,
the hunger never stops;
still i crave

alone in the woods-
where a woman
is no different than a deer.
they'll shoot us both dead
and tear the dignity
from our bones.

we are all just animals,
some cursed by the food chain.
each time i step outside my door,
i am exposed to the darkness
of those woods. victim to invasive
eyes and ass grabs and sneers
with evil plans to display my head
on the wall as a prize to be won.
just another nameless headline,
a statistic with no justice.

do animals pray? are they worthy
of divine intervention? why me, god?
why was i cursed with a womb
and breasts that doom me
from birth? i would gladly eject
them from my body if it meant
that i would go unnoticed,
invisible to predators and
hunters with sinful eyes.

previously published in the 2025
Experiences in Femininity exhibit

black widow,
an emotional masochist

blood of pomegranates drip
from the bones of my spine,
as you rub salt in my wounds.
i mistake it for sugar, for
gentleness. my teeth sinking
into the sickness of your flesh,
to preserve what we once had.
a violent expression of desire,
my love for you is murderous.
i'll spoon feed my heart to you-
but you use a rusted knife.
euphoria in shades of purple
and blue, bruised by that
summer. liquor in your
veins, holy water of our
midnight mistakes with
an everlasting longing.
perhaps i am an emotional
masochist, addicted to the
toxins of someone as sick as you.

the fruits of her bittersweet sadness, left to rot

the fruits of her bittersweet sadness, left to rot

the fruits of her bittersweet sadness, left to rot

dearest reader,

i am eternally grateful for how this book found its way into your tender palms, whether that be from a thrift store bookshelf, a cardboard box in your mailbox, or a gift from a loved one. this collection features some of the most raw, vulnerable pieces i have ever written. it took guts in order to share them with you, so please do be gentle with my heart. this book is for the lost, the ashamed, the lonely. for the dreamers, the poets, the human. enjoy this book in the silence of your childhood bedroom, beneath a willow tree in the evening, in the bathtub over a glass of wine, or balanced on the cat in your lap. if you are starving for more writing like this, my first poetry collection, "when summer fades to fall," is available online.

special thanks to my dearest friend since eighth grade, sadie rose, for illustrating this collection. you brought my ideas to life with such a keen attention to detail, and this piece wouldn't be nearly as bearable without your heart plastered throughout the pages. my lovely birthday twin, i look forward to watching you further grow in your art.

with love, always

leta iris

leta iris (she/they) is a bisexual, two-spirited midwestern poet studying english, with a concentration in creative nonfiction and a minor in creative writing. she is the author of two poetry collections, *when summer fades to fall* and *the fruits of her bittersweet sadness, left to rot.* her piece, "animals," was previously featured in the *Experiences of Femininity* exhibit at the University of Nebraska at Omaha. leta has also been published in several other small literary magazines, such as *South Broadway Press* and *Apotheca Journal.* leta takes pride in her cherokee/apache heritage, with her indigenous name meaning *cheerful spirit.* she enjoys caffeine, thrifting trinkets and collecting purses. you can usually find her beneath a fuzzy blanket, book in hand while cuddled up with her lifelong partner, cody, and her blue-heeler beagle mix, buffy. all writing is original work by leta iris, and may not be used without permission. for business inquiries, email authorletairis@gmail.com <3 stay in the loop of what is coming next through her instagram! @tangledflxwers

sadie rose (she/her) is a sapphic artist from the countryside of new england, focusing on animal portraits of woodland creatures and equines. most days, you will find her in the barn, sketching in her journals while tending to her horses. she often stores carrots in her back pockets, offering the gentle giants a snack as a gift. sadie enjoys painting, exploring the woods on horseback, and drowning out the noise of the world with music. you can follow along on her art and equestrian journey on instagram! @carouselhorsess

all interior artwork is original work by sadie rose and may not be used without permission.

the fruits of her bittersweet sadness, left to rot

the fruits of her bittersweet sadness, left to rot